·····In·Time·of·Need·····

Famine
and Drought

by Sean Connolly

FRANKLIN WATTS
LONDON·SYDNEY

An Appleseed Editions book

First published in 2004 by Franklin Watts
96 Leonard Street, London, EC2A 4XD

Franklin Watts Australia
45–51 Huntley Street, Alexandria, NSW 2015

© 2004 Appleseed Editions

Created by Appleseed Editions Ltd,
Well House, Friars Hill, Guestling, East Sussex, TN35 4ET

Designed by Ian Butterworth

ISBN 0 7496 5711 1

A CIP catalogue for this book is available from the British Library.

Photographs by:
AP/Wide World Photos, Corbis (AFP, Bettmann,
Louise Gubb/CORBIS SABA, Layne Kennedy, Neal Preston,
Chris Rainier, Steve Raymer, Reuters, Peter Turnley), JLM Visuals,
Photodisc, Tom Stack & Associates, Unicorn Stock Photography

Printed in the USA

Contents

What Is Famine?

We have all felt hungry when we were late for a meal or missed a chance to eat. Now imagine how it must feel to miss another meal, and then another, and another. After a while you find that your family not only has no food, but also no way of finding it. The uncomfortable feeling of being hungry becomes much worse, and you find it hard to do the simplest things because you are so tired. And then you realise that you are becoming seriously ill. That is what life is like for people who face **famine.**

A famine is a severe shortage of food that affects people in a large area. It usually affects people who earn their living by farming. The word comes from the Latin *fames*, which means 'hungry.' People have suffered famines for thousands of years – even the ancient Romans experienced famine. Despite many improvements in farming, transport, and food preservation, millions of people are still affected by famine.

Above: When a country faces famine, adults and children alike suffer from severe hunger, fatigue, and illness.

The Causes of Famine

Food scientists make a distinction between widespread hunger and famine. Although people in many countries face regular shortages of food in periods leading up to harvest time, the harvest usually produces enough supplies for the rest of the year. If the weather in the growing season is too wet or too dry, then the next harvest might be affected. People then go through a longer period of hunger – but they can still look forward to the following year's harvest.

A famine, on the other hand, upsets the whole cycle of planting, harvesting and storing extra food. Many things can destroy a harvest and make it impossible to plant new crops, such as **drought**, floods, earthquakes and attacks by insects or other plant-eating pests. People can also trigger famine through wars and other conflicts that destroy farmland and force people off the land.

'Early warning signs were there in abundance. Time and again, women had the same tale to tell. When last year's harvest failed, their families sold their livestock in order to buy food and fresh seed. The rain did not fall, and the crops did not fully develop. By selling their only **assets**, these people have been able to cope until now. But to do so, they are using up all their **resources**.'

World Food Programme Director Catherine Bertini on the 2000 famine in north-east Africa

Below: Without food to eat, livestock also suffer the effects of famine and drought.

'Sometimes my children sit outside and cry from hunger. Sometimes they put a pan on the fire as if expecting me to cook. I tell them there is nothing. After that, all I can do is sit there helplessly and watch them cry.'
Madyawako Lepu, a mother from Malawi, hit by southern Africa's 2002 famine

The Effects of Famine

The main effect of a famine is, of course, hunger. People begin to lose weight and strength, and children do not grow properly. Any person who goes without enough food for a long time begins to suffer **malnutrition**. Over time, this condition becomes very serious and can lead to death by starvation. Hungry, weakened people are also less able to fight off other diseases. Many people in famine regions die from illnesses such as measles, which are not fatal for a healthy person.

The effects of a famine extend often far beyond the immediate farming areas. People with enough strength try to move away from the affected area to places that might have more food. About 1.6 million people left Ireland for other countries during the Irish Famine of 1845–46. More recent famines in Africa have caused similar mass movements of people. During a famine in the 1980s in West Africa, the population of Mauritania's capital city, Nouakshott, grew to four times the population before the famine. Such sudden increases in population can cause many problems for cities and countries that are not equipped to provide food, water and shelter for so many additional people.

Above: An emergency feeding center in Ethiopia. Opposite: These two men are waiting by food supplies in a Sudanese refugee camp, where the Red Cross delivered aid to nearly 150 million Africans during the famine of 1984–85.

GIFT OF THE
EUROPEAN
ECONOMIC COMMUNITY
ACTION OF THE LEAGUE OF
RED CROSS SOCIETIES
FREE DISTRIBUTION

GI
EU
ECONOMIC
ACTION OF T
THE RED CROS
FOR FREE DIS

Drought

It takes a major disturbance to completely destroy a harvest over a wide range of farmland. One of the most common and most destructive famine 'triggers' is drought. We hear the term 'drought' almost every summer because it refers to a long dry period in an area that normally has regular rainfall. People in many countries experience droughts when there is no rain for weeks on end. Lawns turn brown, and water levels dip in some lakes and **reservoirs**. Usually it is only a short drought, and the rain returns after a little time. For many parts of the world, though, a drought can last much longer and have far more serious effects.

One important feature of a drought is that it takes place where people have come to expect and rely on water. In some parts of the world, people have adjusted to periods without rain even longer than most droughts because their

Scientists have learned that six or seven centuries ago, whole areas of the south-west United States were abandoned by Native American farming people because of repeated droughts.

Above: Without regular rainfall, farmers in many parts of the world must rely on irrigation systems to keep their crops alive.

regions have a very dry **climate.** Farmers in northern Mexico, north Africa, central Australia and many parts of Asia know that it may not rain for nearly a year. Knowing this, they plant crops that do not need a great deal of water. They may also set up water pipelines and dig deep wells to **irrigate** their dry lands. But people who face a drought did not expect to go without rain, and have not made any preparations. They can only watch as their corn, wheat and other crops wither and dry on the stalk.

El Niño

El Niño (the Spanish word for 'boy') is the name given to a change in the world's weather pattern that often leads to drought. It develops when currents in the Pacific Ocean that flow past the west coast of South America switch direction. The changing currents cause drought by reducing rainfall near the equator. Unusually warm water also kills fish and other sea life along the coast, making it hard for fishing families in Peru and other countries to feed themselves.

Above: Because droughts can happen unexpectedly, farmers are not always prepared to irrigate, and crops can be destroyed.

A Long
History

Stories and descriptions of famine go back as far as written history. Accounts in the Bible, as well as similar religious records in Asia, tell of sudden periods of extreme hunger affecting a region. The Biblical plague of locusts in Egypt, for example, did not harm humans directly. But by eating the Egyptian grain, the locusts destroyed the harvest and caused many Egyptians to starve.

Different Causes

The plague of locusts in the Bible is one of the earliest accounts of famine that we have. Scientists who study the history of food and **nutrition** agree that there have been about 400 major famines since that time. Some of these famines were man-made – the result of warfare or other disturbances – but most came about because of natural

Above: Infestations of insects, such as locusts, can damage crops and lead to famine.
Left: A 14th century illustration of the Biblical locust plague in Egypt.

causes. Each of these causes is connected to the basic needs of growing plants – good soil, light and water. The most common cause of famine is a shortage of water due to drought.

Asia, in particular, has been the site of many periods of mass starvation because of drought. Experts now estimate that 10 million people died during India's drought in 1769 and 1770. A severe drought caused a similar number of deaths during the famine of 1877 and 1888 in northern China. Severe famines in Africa in the 1970s and 1980s were also linked to drought.

Sometimes a country might lose a single crop and still face a famine, although its other crops are unaffected. That is what happened in Ireland in the 1840s. Most Irish farmers owned very small fields. Potatoes were the only crop that would provide enough food to feed their families within such a small area. In 1845, a tiny potato-blight **fungus** destroyed a whole year's potato harvest. Before long, Ireland faced a terrible famine. Between 1845 and 1851, the population of Ireland dropped from 8.5 million to about 6.5 million.

'Famine is the ultimate public health catastrophe. It is unfortunately a recurrent human phenomenon, even in modern times. Since the end of World War II (1945), there has not been one year in which there was not a famine.'
Jean Mayer, president of Tufts University and an expert on nutrition

Below: An illustration depicting Irish peasants during the 19th century potato famine that resulted in millions of deaths.

Force of
Nature?

Many people consider famines to be unavoidable disasters. In their view, a famine is no easier to prevent or predict than, for example, an earthquake or volcanic eruption. This view considers a famine to be a 'force of nature' or an 'act of God' – something that 'just happens'.

Other people take a different view. Although they accept that natural events can occur without warning, they also believe that people's actions can create or prolong famines. One obvious example is warfare. Widespread fighting can force farmers off their land for one or more harvests. It can also destroy buildings and equipment that farmers need to survive. Constant fighting in the east

Above: International peacekeeping troops entered war-torn Somalia in December 1992 to provide aid as part of 'Operation Restore Hope.' Left: Natural disasters such as volcanic eruptions can sometimes lead to drought and famine.

African country of Somalia in 1992 led to general hunger and even famine there. Peacekeeping troops from the United Nations (UN) helped bring some order to the country. Soon afterwards, the hungriest people were receiving food aid and beginning to rebuild their lives.

Sometimes, a government will force its people to change the way they live and farm. Experts now believe that 7 to 10 million people died in the Ukraine during the early 1930s, when **Soviet** leader Joseph Stalin forced families to leave their farms and move on to new, giant farms. Stalin's program of **communal** farms disguised a deliberate **genocide** that aimed to silence resistance to his government. The opposite has happened over the past five years in Zimbabwe. There, Prime Minister Robert Mugabe has forced many white farmers (who produce much of the country's food) off their large farms. The farms have been divided and given to other farmers, who have neither the money nor the experience to produce the same amount of food.

Below: A worker washes coffee beans – an important cash crop – in Brazil, the world's largest coffee producer and exporter.

'Three months after the aid arrived, three months after the peacekeepers had arrived, there were no more walking skeletons. Many lives were saved, and many people were helped.'
UN Secretary-General Kofi Annan, referring to the 1992 UN peacekeeping mission in war-torn Somalia, where famine loomed

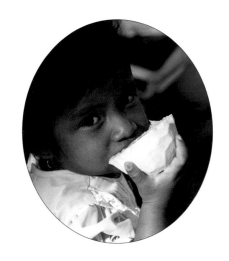

CASH CROPS

Sometimes, the best farmland in a country is used to produce 'cash crops' – food or goods that are exported to other countries – rather than crops that the country needs to feed itself. The choice of crops often depends on the country's government. For example, China has more than twice as many people for each acre of farmland as many other countries. Yet people in China are not hungry, whereas as many as 70 percent of the children in Central America and the Caribbean are UNDERNOURISHED. At least half of the farmland in these regions – usually the best land – is used to grow crops such as coffee and cocoa for export, instead of food for the local people.

ONE FAMILY'S TRAGEDY

Madyawako Lepu, part of a farming family in Malawi, lost her husband in March 2002. He was buried in the new village graveyard along with many of their neighbours. 'We had no food at all and eventually my husband started to swell,' Madyawako said, holding the youngest of her seven children. 'In desperation, we started eating banana roots and other wild plants, which we had never eaten before. But it was not enough to save my husband.'

Focus on
Africa

Africa has many of the conditions that can contribute to severe hunger and famine: unreliable rains and flooding, wars and harsh governments. But the primary reason that Africa suffers is because most of its people are poor and unable to build up stocks of food and grain to support themselves during hard times. In the 1980s and 1990s, there were terrible famines in the west African region known as the Sahel (just south of the Sahara Desert), as well as in Ethiopia and neighbouring east African countries.

Above: The great poverty caused by famine and drought can force some people into slave labour as a means of survival.

The Latest Famine

By mid-2002, it was becoming clear that another famine was looming in southern Africa. The countries affected most were Malawi, Zimbabwe, Swaziland, Mozambique, Lesotho and Zambia. As with previous African famines, a deadly combination of natural and man-made causes lay behind the severe shortage of food. Heavy flooding in 2000 and 2001 had ruined many farms. Then, an unusually harsh dry spell affected crops planted in preparation for the next harvest. In addition to these problems, southern Africa had been hit harder by **AIDS** than anywhere else in the world. Many people in farming communities died, and others were seriously ill themselves or caring for those who were affected. This made it particularly difficult to cope with the reduced harvests.

Above: Patients sit outside the Tshupe Hospice for terminally ill AIDS patients in Rustenburg, South Africa.

THE MENACE OF AIDS

The terrible medical condition known as **AIDS** (Acquired Immune Deficiency Syndrome) is caused by infection with a virus called **HIV**. It affects the body's ability to fight off other diseases. People do not die from **AIDS** itself, but from the infections that AIDS allows to develop – influenza, pneumonia, and even the common cold.

Southern Africa has a severe **AIDS** problem, which contributed to the recent food crisis. In Swaziland, nearly one person in three has been infected. Many adults have died, leaving their children with no one to look after them. Phumephi Shongwe, whose parents died of **AIDS**, sums up the story for thousands of children in the region. 'Every time my stomach hurts from hunger, it reminds me of my parents. It wouldn't be happening if they were still alive. My father was not a wealthy man, but he always managed to provide for us.'

NOTHING TO CELEBRATE

Food shortages and famine have had other, less obvious effects on life in southern Africa. In many villages in Malawi, Swaziland and Zambia, there have been no weddings or similar ceremonies at all for a year or more. The reason is simple: there is no food to spare for celebrations.

There were also problems with the way that some countries in southern Africa managed their **reserves** of grain and food. Malawi had very small supplies of seeds and **fertilisers**, and had sold much of its grain reserves even before the problems began. Then, when farmers began suffering, the government delayed buying grain from other countries. 'I was fortunate because I kept enough seeds to plant,' said 77-year old farmer Zakeyo Mose. 'But the maize corn is much smaller than usual, and it will not last beyond September.' It is often difficult to recover from a famine because the seeds needed for planting have been eaten. Even if there are enough seeds to plant, the simple task of planting has become almost impossible because people have lost so much strength and energy to hunger.

Above: Cattle are herded on a previously white-owned farm near Centenary, Zimbabwe. The farm is now occupied by formerly landless Zimbabweans who do not have enough money to run a successful farming operation.

Southern Africa's problems have been made worse by the political situation in Zimbabwe. In recent years, the government has seized white-owned farms and stopped farmers from importing grain, causing a shortage. Zimbabwe was once called the 'bread basket' of the region because it produced so much food. Neighbouring countries relied on its **surplus** food for their own survival.

Above: In Zimbabwe, political chaos and violence have crippled the nation, causing severe famine and drought. In May 2003, Zimbabwean President Robert Mugabe (right) and President Bakili Muluzi of Malawi (left) met with South African President Thabo Mbeki and Nigerian President Olusegun Obasanjo for intense negotiations aimed at bringing peace to Zimbabwe.

'Lots of people come here and beg, and it is very difficult to say no when women come with crying babies. But I also have a family to feed. So sometimes I say yes and sometimes I say no, but it is always a hard decision. I cannot remember it ever being this bad.'
Kate Mose, describing life in her village in Malawi

Africa now produces nearly 30 percent less food per person than it did in 1967.

Reaching the
Hungry

Although a famine can develop as a result of a sudden event such as an earthquake or a major battle, it usually takes effect gradually. The problem worsens if the people governing a region fail to notice some of the warning signs, such as dwindling supplies of grain, sun-baked soil, or even farmers too weak to work. The famine begins to gather speed as each growing problem makes the other problems worse.

Above: During a famine, it is critical to get food rations to children so they grow up strong and healthy. Left: Schoolchildren facing starvation due to a drought in Zimbabwe line up for food supplied by the United Nations World Food Program.

It is important to deliver emergency food aid quickly. Pregnant women in particular need to be well-nourished. Scientists have shown that babies born to undernourished mothers do not grow properly in later life. This means that even if emergency food arrives in time to keep people alive, the famine will have long-term effects. Children will grow up weaker and less healthy. Most importantly, they will be less able to deal with the same hardships that led to the first famine. This 'hunger trap' can form a terrible cycle that is hard to break.

Recognising the Problem

It is important to recognise the problem and act as soon as possible. The best people to make this judgment are those in charge of a region's government. During the famine that developed in Malawi in 2002, it became clear at harvest time that the corn harvest was nowhere near enough to feed the population. President Bakili Muluzi declared a **state of emergency**, which drew attention to the crisis. Other governments have taken similar steps over the years, often looking to the outside world for help. Recognition of the problem is the first stage of famine relief.

Malawian President Bakili Muluzi, shown here voting in his country's 1999 democratic elections, has worked to draw attention to the impoverished condition of the Malawian people.

Emergency Action

It is important that famine relief is distributed sensibly and fairly. Local officials must decide which regions are worst hit, and which are most likely to be in immediate danger. This helps them to send relief where it is needed most. Relief generally comes in three forms.

First, the hungry people need food and drink. Famine relief workers must know which types of food are best for the local conditions. Vitamin supplements and high-protein biscuits help restore some of the essential nutrition that famine sufferers have lost. Workers must also ensure that the food reaches those who are too weak to walk to the emergency camps they have set up. Relief workers aim to supply regular amounts of wheat and other grains to those who need them. The World Food Program recommends 15 kilograms of wheat per person per month.

Governments, both local and foreign, often join forces with international aid agencies to provide and distribute emergency food supplies. Getting these supplies to remote areas can be a problem in countries that have few roads or railroad lines. During Ethiopia's food crisis in 2000, for example, other countries flew in vehicles and fuel to help distribute food and medical goods.

Above: A young boy kisses the hand of World Food Program Executive Director Catherine Bertini. Left: North Korean workers sort high-protein biscuits at a factory supported by the World Food Program.

The second form of relief aid consists of medical supplies and experienced health workers who can treat some of the diseases linked to famine, such as malnutrition. Last, but just as important, relief workers must supply local farmers with new stocks of seeds so that they can plant new crops. This last measure is the first step towards avoiding another famine. Until the crops are harvested, local people must rely on regular supplies of emergency food aid.

Below: Local residents load sacks of food donated by the Red Cross for distribution at a village in North Korea.

'The situation here is very, very bad. But [relief groups] like us don't have the resources to help all those in need. We can only feed the most vulnerable families – the very poorest of the poor.'
William Kelly of Caritas, an organization that distributes food aid in Lokhayiza, Swaziland

'With this food aid – the maize, beans and vegetable oil – we're going to make it even though it will still be hard. If the food stops coming, then people are going to die.'
Vusi Shangabu, describing famine conditions in eastern Swaziland

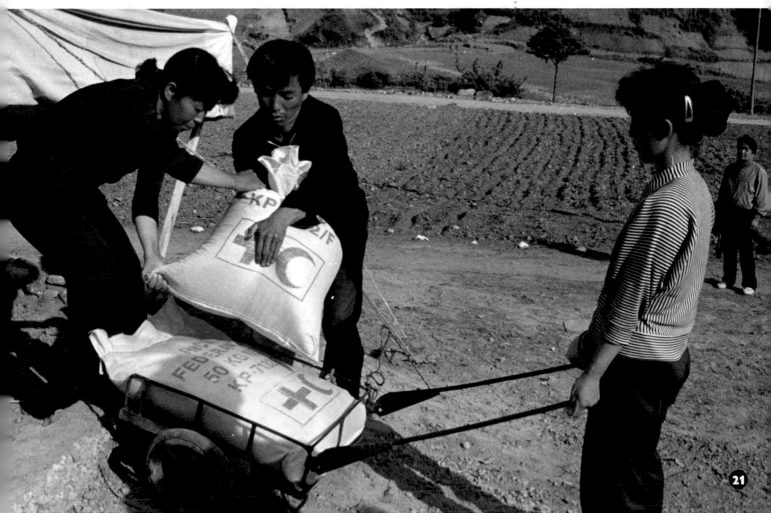

The World
Reacts

Other disasters, such as hurricanes, earthquakes, landslides and floods, can kill hundreds or even thousands of people. Any loss of life is terrible, but a single famine can lead to millions of deaths in a country or region. In a world of instant news, it is impossible to ignore the suffering of so many human beings. Countries, groups of countries and international organizations respond each time there is news of a famine occurring anywhere in the world. They try to send emergency supplies and experienced relief workers to help the affected countries.

Some wealthy countries use government money to pay for famine relief around the world. Goverments of the developed countries, such as the members of the European

Above: A homeless man sits in front of graffiti in Johannesburg, South Africa. International aid organizations try to prevent the poverty and homelessness that can result from a prolonged famine.

Union, the United States, Canada and Australia, frequently respond to calls for help. These nations, whether working on their own or together, are called **donor** nations.

The international community, led by the United Nations, also plays an important role in dealing with the problems of famine. The United Nations was formed just after World War II ended in 1945. Two UN organisations – the United Nations Relief and Rehabilitation Administration and the Food and Agriculture Organisation (FAO) – were created soon afterwards. The goal of these organisations is to deal with the problem of hunger and food shortages around the world. In 1963, the United Nations set up another organisation, the World Food Program (WFP), to focus on famine and other critical food problems. The WFP coordinates relief efforts in famine-affected regions and appeals to UN member-countries for contributions. For example, in 2002, the WFP mounted a £300 million appeal to feed 10.2 million people in southern Africa.

THE 30-HOUR FAMINE

One of the most imaginative famine-relief efforts is the 30-Hour Famine, established by the American Christian group World Vision. Groups of young volunteers raise money from sponsors to help starving children in some of the world's poorest countries. The groups then go without food for 30 hours, so that they can have a real sense of what hunger is like. During this time they take part in a range of local activities before collecting their money and sending it to World Vision projects in Latin America, Africa, and Asia.

Above: World Food Program Executive Director Catherine Bertini and WFP spokesperson Trevor Rowe talk with a group of Rwandan children who are returning to their homes after being forced to leave several years earlier because of a civil war.

'Thank you for loving your neighbours halfway across the world.'
E.A. Kayange, Coordinator of 30-Hour Famine Funds in Magole, Tanzania

LIVE AID

A **BBC** news broadcast from famine-affected Africa in 1984 inspired Irish pop singer **Bob Geldof** to create a special project to help famine victims. Geldof persuaded many other singers to form a special band, called **Band Aid**, to record the song 'Do They Know It's Christmas'. In 1985, American singers formed a similar band called **USA for Africa** to record the song 'We Are the World'. All the money from the sales of the two records went to African famine relief.

These records earned huge sums of money, so Geldof went a stage further. On July 13, 1985, he organized Live Aid, a special televised concert that took place at the same time in London and Philadelphia. The singers performed for free while volunteers took telephone pledges from millions of people who watched the 16-hour concert. Live Aid was a great success and continues to collect money from people around the world. By 2002, it had raised more than US $100 million.

Relief Organizations

In addition to the UN organizations, a number of other international groups help out in times of famine. The oldest of these is the International Federation of Red Cross and Red Crescent Societies originally founded in Switzerland in 1864. Like the UN, the Red Cross organises relief efforts both within and between countries. Many religious groups, such as Christian Aid, the World Jewish Congress and Caritas, also raise funds and send supplies in times of famine.

Above and opposite: Artists and organisers gather on stage for the finale of the Live Aid concert.

Below: A volunteer from the One Love Children's Project dishes bowls of curry and rice to the homeless people of South Africa. Twice a week, homeless men, women and children gather for meals provided by the self-funded project.

HEADING OFF DONOR FATIGUE

One of the problems faced by disaster relief organisers is 'donor fatigue'. People sometimes lose interest in giving money because there seems to be no end to the bad news. International figures, such as UN Secretary-General Kofi Annan, try to prevent this 'fatigue' from affecting much-needed relief efforts.

After 435,000 tonnes of food was pledged to Africa in 2000, Annan was asked whether donor nations may be becoming 'fatigued' by Africa's many disasters. He answered: 'The fatigue may be there, but I don't think we can justify it in the face of such misery. We may need to wake up our CONSCIENCE and our conscience must force us to act.'

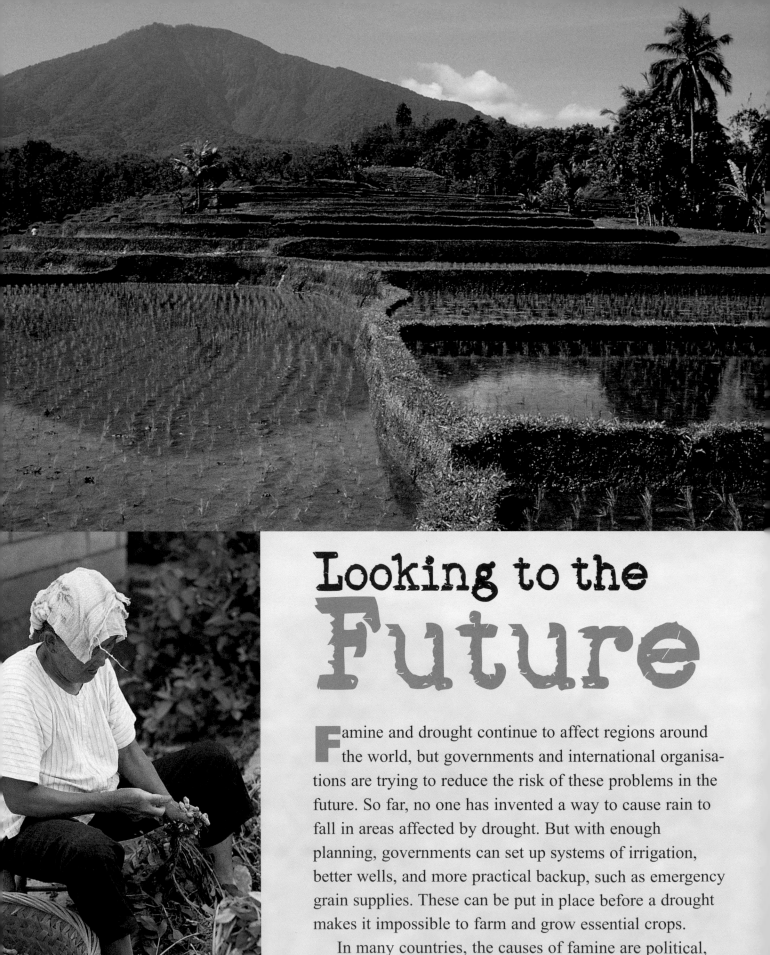

Looking to the
Future

Famine and drought continue to affect regions around the world, but governments and international organisations are trying to reduce the risk of these problems in the future. So far, no one has invented a way to cause rain to fall in areas affected by drought. But with enough planning, governments can set up systems of irrigation, better wells, and more practical backup, such as emergency grain supplies. These can be put in place before a drought makes it impossible to farm and grow essential crops.

In many countries, the causes of famine are political, not natural. These problems are harder to tackle. People in

Above: Rice paddies in Indonesia provide hope for a fruitful harvest. Left: This woman is harvesting peanuts in China, a heavily populated country that has almost completely eliminated the threat of famine through preparation and planning.

such countries go hungry because the systems of land ownership and choices about which crops to grow are insufficient to feed the people properly. It can be difficult to change such widespread systems.

Improving Conditions

There have been some success stories in many countries over the past 100 years. Famine affected China in the 1920s, but it is no longer a problem there. The Chinese people have built reservoirs and greatly increased the amount of their irrigated land in preparation for drought. As a result, harvests of important grains are double what they once were. China has also led the way in **birth control**, making sure that the population does not increase faster than the country's ability to feed its people.

India faced famine in the 1940s, but most of the country is free of famine today. India's approach has been described as a 'green revolution'. The government encouraged farmers to use types of crops that would thrive, and farmers began to rely more on fertilisers and irrigation. Although people in some parts of India still face hunger, today the country as a whole is **self-sufficient**.

A Better Future?

With the rapid growth in use of the Internet, cellular phones and satellite communications, information can be sent across the world and received in seconds. People have begun to describe the world as a 'global village'. Instant communication may help to solve the problem of famine by giving individuals and governments more warning about people who need food urgently. Local officials may be able to alert the wider world as soon as problems arise. Donor countries and international aid agencies may use high-speed communications to deliver food shipments smoothly and efficently.

At the beginning of the 21st century, scientists announced that the world was producing more than enough food for the more than six billion people on the planet. They also believed that current methods of farming

INDIA'S GRAND PLAN

New farming methods in the 20th century had nearly put an end to India's serious hunger concerns. But with its population of more than one billion growing by thousands each day, the government is worried about producing enough food to feed all its people. India has some of the driest – and wettest – regions of any country. In November 2002, Indian Prime Minister Atal Bihari Vajpayee announced plans for a huge plan to transfer water from India's wettest regions to its driest. The project, which involves building many canals, dams and reservoirs, will cost billions of pounds. The Prime Minister said that the improvements would 'change the destiny of the country' by ending its water problems for good.

would allow us to continue to feed the world's growing population in the decades to come. But although there is enough food, it may not be in the right place at the right time.

Many people in the world do not have enough land on which to grow crops, or cannot afford to buy enough food. To address this problem, many developing countries are following the example of India's 'green revolution' by focusing on improved methods of irrigating land and harvesting crops. New strains of grains and other crops have been developed that can produce more food with each harvest – as long as farmers have access to seeds.

The Food and Agriculture Organisation has made many recommendations to combat – and possibly overcome – hunger.

- An international system of fair trade should ensure that poorer countries can sell their crops at a good price.

- The international community should promote peace.

- Governments should make an extra effort to protect clean air and water, farmland and other natural resources.

- Wealth should be distributed more equally to enable everyone to be able to produce or buy their own food.

- Women, who produce half of the world's food but own only one percent of its land, should have equal rights.

- Farmers should rediscover forgotten foods: some hungry people are unaware of nourishing foods that their ancestors had eaten.

- Land reform should be enacted to give small farmers a better chance.

- There should be a 'blue revolution' – we should get more of our food from the sea.

Of course, not all of these changes will take place overnight. But with a combined effort from rich and poor countries alike, the world should be able to defeat famine.

Opposite: Fish sellers bring in their fresh catch in southern India. Part of overcoming hunger in years to come will most likely include a heavier reliance on harvesting food from the sea.

Glossary

AIDS Acquired Immune Deficiency Syndrome, a condition that makes it hard for the body to fight off diseases

assets property that can be sold or used to buy other goods

birth control various methods that can be used to limit the number of children in a single family

climate the average weather for a particular place

communal shared, rather than private, ownership

conscience a sense of what is right and wrong

developing countries countries, mainly in Africa, Asia and Latin America, that have few industries

donor a person or country that gives money or something else of value freely to another person or country

drought a long period with no rain

famine a serious shortage of food in a large area

fertilisers nutrients added to the soil to make it produce more and better crops

fungus a form of life, such as mushrooms and mould, that resembles plants but does not need light to grow

genocide the deliberate killing of a nation or similar large group of people

HIV Human Immunovirus, the tiny, nonliving parasite, or virus, that causes AIDS

irrigate to transport water to dry farmland

malnutrition a weakened condition caused by not eating enough nutritious food for a long time

nutrition the amount and type of food that a person eats; or the study of how the body needs and uses food

reserves amounts of something useful that are held back for use in a crisis

reservoirs bodies of fresh water created to provide drinking water or to irrigate crops

resources things that can be used to take care of a need

self-sufficient not needing any outside help; able to support itself

Soviet having to do with the Soviet Union, a country formed by Russia, Ukraine, and 13 other nations from 1917 to 1991

state of emergency a government declaration that results in extra help to an area facing a disaster

surplus more than is needed; extra

undernourished not getting enough nutritious food

Further Reading

Books

Visual Factfinder: Planet Earth,
by Neil Curtis and Michael Allaby.
London: Grisewood and Dempsey, 1993.

The Usborne Book of Weather Facts,
by Anita Ganeri.
London: Usborne, 1992.

Web sites

Medicins Sans Frontieres
www.msf.org

International Committee of the Red Cross and
Red Crescent (ICRC)
www.icrc.org

Melbourne Water (Australia)
http://Drought.melbournewater.com.au

Australian Environmental Education Network
http://www.environment.gov.au/education/aeen/

Index